How to Manage
Disruptive Change

How to Manage Disruptive Change

Leadership | Vision | Technology | Talent

Bob Shafto

ARCHWAY
PUBLISHING

Archway Publishing books may be ordered through booksellers or by contacting:

Archway Publishing
1663 Liberty Drive
Bloomington, IN 47403
www.archwaypublishing.com
1 (888) 242-5904

Because of the dynamic nature of the Internet, any web addresses or links contained in this book may have changed since publication and may no longer be valid. The views expressed in this work are solely those of the author and do not necessarily reflect the views of the publisher, and the publisher hereby disclaims any responsibility for them.

Any people depicted in stock imagery provided by Getty Images are models, and such images are being used for illustrative purposes only. Certain stock imagery © Getty Images.

This book is a work of non-fiction. Unless otherwise noted, the author and the publisher make no explicit guarantees as to the accuracy of the information contained in this book and in some cases, names of people and places have been altered to protect their privacy.

ISBN: 978-1-4808-7125-0 (sc)
ISBN: 978-1-4808-7123-6 (hc)
ISBN: 978-1-4808-7124-3 (e)

Library of Congress Control Number: 2018913937

Print information available on the last page.

Archway Publishing rev. date: 1/7/2019

CONTENTS

INTRODUCTION

The overwhelming questions of our time are:

- Can today's organizations learn to adapt to accelerating change?
- Do they have the necessary leadership skills?
- Can they overcome their personal and organizational bias for the status quo?
- Can they win the talent war?
- Can they successfully meet the demands of today's empowered workforce and customers?
- Can they manage the challenges of digital transformation and cybersecurity?
- Can they embrace change and become an adaptive organization?

With the view that accelerating change is making the future impossible to plan for and with a clear sense of the long-term nature of organizations, this book offers a repository of ideas, concepts, and principles for organizational debate, discussion, and decision-making. It views uncertainty as an opportunity to create a competitive advantage.

The premise is that organizations need to think differently, rethink everything, and create an adaptive symmetry of leadership, vision, technology, and talent.

The future, by its nature, is unpredictable, without definition, shape, form, or boundaries—ambiguous, difficult to understand, and easily misinterpreted. Our reactions can swing back and forth inconsistently, divided and hesitating.

In an environment of disruptive change, strategic planning as we know it is no longer workable. Accelerating change makes the future less knowable and impossible to plan for.

Organizations need to become flexible, resilient, and innovative. They need to learn to adjust to constantly changing circumstances and situations. They need to become adaptive.

Imagine that you are the CEO, meeting in the conference room with the leadership team discussing the business challenges facing the organization. Each team member brings to the table divergent perspectives and points of view about the issues. You are responsible for making the decisions that lead to a major change in direction. You need to frame the right questions, listen, and seek out uncomfortable opinions and ideas. Say to the executive committee, "Tell me what you think I do not want to hear."

The candid discussion then leads to comments from members of the leadership team about recent headlines from Bloomberg, the *Wall Street Journal*, *Forbes*, and the *Harvard Business Review*: "Tracking the Slow Decline of American Icons"; "Surviving a Quickly Changing World"; "Revenue Decline Continues"; "Companies Fail at Digital Transformation"; "Department Store Sales Slide"; "Rating Companies Give Close Scrutiny to Shopping Malls"; "Unraveling of the Retail Sector."

As CEO, listening to opinions and suggestions can uncover hidden problems and opportunities, leading you to perspective-shifting conclusions.

This is a story about people facing ambiguity and uncertainty, learning to discover the vital few out of the trivial many, thinking outside the box where one idea leads to another—exploring, adapting, evolving, creating, innovating, and problem-solving in an environment of disruptive change.

It is about the ideas and principles of becoming an adaptive enterprise. It is about leadership and followers preparing today for tomorrow. It is about influencing and leading organizational change.

The Greek philosopher Heraclitus was famous for his insistence on ever-present change as being the fundamental essence of the universe. Change is part of everyday life, but few would disagree that today "everything is changing, and the rate of change is accelerating."

The demographics are changing; the millennial's think differently. Customer satisfaction, perceptions, and requirements continue to get redefined. Competitors and markets are changing. Apple, Amazon, Facebook, Microsoft, and Alphabet, the parent company of Google, are growing. New technologies as seen in drones, self-driving cars, artificial intelligence, cognitive computing, 3-D printers, specialized computing with task-focused chips, virtual reality, the internet, cloud computing, software as a service, fiber optics, mobile, networks, and cybersecurity are changing. Shopping preferences and internet retailing result in vacant mall space. Governmental policies, international trade, entertainment, big media, advertising, and healthcare are all changing.

The constantly evolving landscape of accelerating change is redefining all the rules of business. When the future and thus the business environment were more stable, top management used an annual strategic planning process to express the organization's strategies, actions, goals, and objectives.

The strategic planning document was distributed throughout the organization to set priorities, focus resources, and guide decision-making. Businesses defined, measured, analyzed, and controlled for problem-solving, and they emphasized the importance of customer satisfaction. However, the business plans, the well-defined organizational structures, the methodologies, processes, policies, and job roles are all highly resistant to change.

Studies show that even in the face of uncertainty and risk, decision-making is biased toward the status quo, the familiar, the earlier decisions, and organizational inertia. However, is the status quo an alternative? Albert Einstein viewed insanity as doing the same thing over and over and expecting a different result.

This book argues that disruptive change is here to stay and that the pressure on today's organizations will only grow more intense. There's universal agreement that a transformational change is needed for long-term growth and survival.

Although challenging, rethinking everything can create opportunities. This book offers a set of management guidelines, principles, concepts, and ideas for rethinking the organization.

Successfully navigating the waves of change needs persuasive communications, a leadership team with a sense of wonder, a tolerance for ambiguity and followers, a new and innovative planning process, and the extensive use of team-based multidiscipline project management techniques throughout the organization.

New human resource programs for internal recognition and external recruiting of change agents and problem-solvers are needed. Moreover, an innovative digital transformation—an adaptive infrastructure—is needed.

Although this book's primary focus is the business enterprise, its board of directors, management, staff, family members, business partners, and suppliers, the concepts and principles apply to healthcare, education, and government entities as well.

CHAPTER 1

Confront Reality of Disruptive Change

The Status Quo Is an Illusion—Not Sustainable

If we could picture disruptive change by graphically displaying the speed (frequency) and the volatility (amplitude), we could appreciate the broad impact of the continually changing range of interrelated causes. We could see that both the speed and volatility are quickening. Today's environment has more disruptive change than at any time in history.

Technology will continue to get smaller, faster, more intelligent, networked, and integrated into everything. As the demographics and the customer requirements, tastes, and behaviors continue to change, so must the products and services that businesses offer.

Research shows that consumer behavior is changing. Many are moving to online retail, not getting married, not having as many children, downsizing their living space, cutting back on purchases, aggressively seeking deals, and preferring fresh and healthier food choices.

For example, for the millennials generation, seventy-three million strong, their primary source of news and information is the internet. They are highly educated and technologically connected and expect businesses to adjust to their needs. They communicate much differently than the earlier generations. The millennials will change the world more than any other generation.

Some businesses have become victims of disruptive change, while the fortunes of others have waxed and waned. Growth markets come and go. Everything has a shelf life.

In today's uncertain business environment, both the threats and the opportunities are accelerating. Albert Einstein said, "Our world is a product of our thinking; it cannot be changed without changing our thinking."

However, humans have been remarkably adaptive to change. We have learned to survive and prosper no matter what life, the environment, or technology throws at us. In our paradoxical world, organizations resist change with a powerful bias for the status quo. Many of us prefer consistency, keeping everything the same, a preference for the current and sticking with decisions made previously. The status quo is frequently used as a reference point for decision-making.

Behavioral science research has found that when faced with complicated issues, we have a mental shortcut that allows us to decide quickly and efficiently, where our current emotions of fear, pleasure, and surprise influence our decisions. In other words, emotions play a leading role when we face multifaceted judgments.

Our emotions rate more involved decisions on a bipolar scale that is good or bad, suggesting that we base many of our judgments not only on what we think about the decision but how we feel about it.

Understanding the heuristic effect, the mental shortcut that allows people to make judgments when dealing with complex problems is central to creating an adaptive organization.

The executive leadership must thoughtfully frame the communications based on how people think and instinctively decide. Clearly articulating the reality of the situation and the choices that influenced the decisions. Employees need to hear an exciting vision of growth and opportunity—a unique, genuine, compelling, and believable story. A story about innovative products and services created by cross-functional project teams. A strategic vision where employees can learn, develop, contribute, and bring value to the organization.

Disruptive change from developments in technology and changing demographics will create new challenges and new opportunities at every turn. The impact of disruptive change will require an organization to think differently and rethink everything.

CHAPTER 2

Adaptive Leadership—Followers

Collective Wisdom—Progressive Realization

Organizations fail when the leadership's focus is on the status quo, the current operational effectiveness and efficiencies, the shareholders' reaction to quarterly earnings, and the traditional top-down strategic planning, control, and decision-making processes. Disruptive change has undermined the effectiveness of conventional strategic planning.

Failure comes from the following:

- not future-proofing the organization
- not creating a resilient business model
- not offering a strategic vision for the horizon

- not understanding:
  - disruptive change
  - digital transformation
  - cybersecurity
- not focusing on talent management and employee satisfaction
- thinking they have all the answers
  - not realizing that the future is discovered through prototyping and experimentation
- not building mutually beneficial business partnerships
- not investing in intangible assets

Strategic decision-making is about choices. The CEO and the leadership team are responsible for setting the organization's direction. In the shadows of doubt and uncertainty, they must find solutions for the impacts of disruptive change, digital transformation, and cybersecurity. So, how can you plan an organizational direction when you cannot predict the outcome of your choices? The answers are adaptive leadership, collective wisdom, an adaptive business model, and a process of experimentation, learning, and discovering.

Today's form of planning involves a process of progressive realization, the concept that knowledge, understanding, and perspectives are transient over time. Progressive realization uses a network of cross-functional teams to design and create alternatives, then test, measure, learn, rethink, and restart.

Adaptive leadership is a style where the CEO encourages sharing, the expression of ideas, and an active participatory role in decision-making. The management team should have unfettered discussions, ask questions, listen, have open dialogues and vigorous debates, challenge assumptions, and think long-term.

The team should avoid underestimating the threats or missed opportunities by narrowly framing the discussions. They should rethink the organization's strengths, weaknesses, and competitive positions. They should be innovative and consider a wide variety of options, then apply their collective wisdom to the risks and opportunities of the choices.

The CEO should consider introducing diverse ways of thinking and different reference points about the choices by adding a chief talent officer, a chief customer officer, and a chief artificial intelligence officer to the leadership team.

With collective wisdom decision-making, the leadership team's combined cognitive differences can create unique permutations and produce new innovative solutions. However, the most important advantage is the management team's shared understanding and a shared commitment to implement the decisions.

How you communicate both the problems of disruptive change and your solutions to the organization matters. The words that you use matter. Framing the decision as an opportunity will create more divergent thinking, more openness to the choices, more creativity, and more adaptive responses.

Today, talent management and employee engagement are essential activities. Introducing a newsletter about "The Adaptive Journey" can help employees better understand the decision-making process, the options considered, the choices, and the future opportunities they offer. A new strategic vision statement will then guide the enterprise's future technologies, innovations, team-based structures, and talent management programs.

The Adaptive Leadership Dilemma—Being Tri-Modal

First, managing disruptive change is not traditional change management. Unlike a reorganization, an acquisition, a new IT project, entering a new market, or offering a new product, with disruptive change, adaptive leaders cannot disseminate a detailed plan to guide the organization through the changes before they start. Managing adaptive change involves recomposing a known solution to the new situation or developing an effective response to the changing circumstances.

Also, adaptive leaders must be agents of disruptive change. Through the constant process of learning, creativity, and innovation, they must proactively seek new approaches, new products, new services, and new ideas. Moreover, adaptive leaders have the responsibility of successfully overseeing the ongoing day-to-day tasks of the organization.

The Adaptive Leader's Perception Engine—Outcomes

The CEO and the leadership team each have their unique backgrounds, perspectives, opinions, cognitive biases, and assumptions. Our perceptions, filtered by our natural competencies, are how we receive and translate our experiences. Our perception engine defines how we feel, think, and act.

The adaptive leader's perception engine is the mind's eye, questioning by nature, continuously analyzing, searching for verbs, and looking for patterns. It identifies the essential components in the unfolding circumstances and evaluates the critical adjustments for performance in the newly evolving environment.

Components of an adaptive leader's perception engine include a tolerance for ambiguity, excepting mistakes within reason, the ability to work with unknowns and the unpredictable, a willingness to give up control to get results, and the skills to find the vital few out of the trivial many.

In today's businesses, the ongoing challenges of disruptive change, long-term growth, and survival require an adaptive organization—one with the capability to adjust to continuously changing situations and circumstances.

Ross Perot, at Electronic Data Systems, would ask new employees, "What is your definition of leadership?" After listening to various explanations, he would say, "The definition of leadership is: they have followers. The question is, Why do they follow?" Again, the new employees had a variety of perspectives about why leaders have followers. Ross would then define the relationship as need based. A successful leader offers perspectives, knowledge, skills, and abilities the followers need. Leaders are persistent, decisive, innovative, and adaptive. They ask questions, listen, and respond. They are visionaries who communicate a clear organizational direction, ralling support, and motivating followers.

Adaptive leadership is not for the fainthearted.

CHAPTER 3

Shared Strategic Vision

A Great Place to Work

Creating an Adaptive Corporate Culture

The CEO and the management team are responsible for the analysis of problematic situations that could challenge the organization's long-term growth and survival.

Disruptive change requires rethinking the organizational emphasis on the short-term competitive advantage, market share, and quarterly earnings. It is ideal to focus instead on long-term sustainability by fully embracing strategies of adaptability, technology, and talent management.

The CEO and the leadership team should create a strategic vision of core beliefs and shared values that describe the corporate culture and guide the enterprise's future decisions.

The process should begin by asking and answering a series of questions:

- What are we good at?
- What do we want to become?
- What do we believe in?
- What do we intend to achieve?
- What talents do we need?
- Why work for us?

As an internal communications document, the strategic vision statement gives the organization a perspective on the path forward and offers a sense of purpose beyond profit maximization.

As part of an employer-branding campaign, the strategic vision statement describes how the organization's culture is different from other competitive employers and why prospective candidates would want to work there. A shared strategic vision with high standards of excellence and a theme of creativity, innovation, learning, and opportunity would engage and inspire both current employees and future candidates.

The new vision statement should describe the organization's strategic goals, such as becoming an adaptive enterprise by winning the talent war.

- We are building the means to adapt to an ever-changing world.
- We are transparent and share information openly.
- We tolerate ambiguity.
- We are not afraid to change.
- We are willing to test new ideas.
- We embrace and celebrate the diversity of minds.
- We actively support our community.
- We look for, hire, and help develop talented people.
- We build leaders from within.
- We thoroughly debate strategy and trust others to execute the tactics.
- We are committed to continual improvement.
- Together, our business partners and talented employee teams collaborate, solve problems, and satisfy customer requirements.
- We will win by exploring avenues of learning, innovation, flexibility, technology, and talent.

An optimistic and positive strategic vision will set a new and exciting organizational direction. It will take away much of the ambivalence and uncertainty that is associated with today's environment. It will differentiate the organization by creating the ability to adjust to constantly changing circumstances and conditions. It will build an architectural symmetry of leadership, vision, technology, and talent in a culture that is prepared for whatever the future brings

The Power of a Shared Strategic Vision

The vision statement is the organization's compass. If well designed, well communicated, well understood, and broadly accepted by the organization, when faced with decisions, all you need to ask is "Does this decision move us in the right direction?" It is like sailing; you know where you want to go, but with the continually shifting wind, tides, water depth, and various hazards, you cannot sail in a straight line. You must tack, continually adapting and resetting your course. Sailing a five-degree wind shift for one minute can lose or gain your organization three boat lengths. As the winds shift, a shared strategic vision can put the enterprise on the lifted or winning tact.

Organizations without a shared vision will get battered by disruptive change and may lose their sense of direction.

CHAPTER 4

Teams, Projects, Project Management, and Facilitation

The Wisdom of Teams

Work Groups versus Teams

Functional work groups are traditional work units or departmental groups with a supervisor who plays an active role, assigns work, answers questions, and measures individual performance. Functional workgroup activities are more repetitive and have a focus on internal or external customer satisfaction. Teams, on the other hand, are both individually and mutually accountable for the team's results; they share information and perspectives, focus on team goals, and aim for a collective work product.

Diversity of Minds over Ability

Business is increasingly becoming an environment where teams work collaboratively. Teams with diverse perspectives, personality traits, talents, backgrounds, and interests are better at innovation, creativity, problem-solving, and decision-making than capable individuals alone or teams with cognitive bias.

With greater diversity will come collective wisdom, task-relevant information, and an array of borrowed perceptions.

Teams do the following:

- view the problem from different angles
- perceive adjacent possibilities
- offer ideas in the neighborhood
- introduce information, knowledge, and wisdom
- propose fresh new solutions

By thinking differently, the whole becomes more significant than the sum of its parts, and outcomes are enhanced.

Assembling Unconventional Teams

Building a project team is about both diversity and ability. Actively seek generalists and specialists as well as people with different experiences, educational and functional backgrounds, cognitive depth, age, and personality traits.

Without a diversity of minds and backgrounds, the project team can become lopsided with cognitive bias. It will be less creative and have fewer innovative ideas.

Assembling an effective project team is not about assigning human resources; it is about the autonomy of thought.

The NeuroColor personality assessments can help an organization assemble diverse project teams that think differently from multifaceted angles.

Team-Based Organizational Structures

Until recently corporate-level strategic planning activities drove strategic business unit (SBU) objectives and in turn directed functional department action plans. These first principles of management, along with the associated skills and abilities, are changing.

Today, organizations have flatter structures and are more team based. Functional departments have started to become less well defined. Team dynamics tend to become multi-directional rather than hierarchical.

The growth of cross-functional teams has influenced both decision-making processes and organizational structures.

Cross-Functional Teams

Technology, talent, and innovation are today's differentiators, and cross-functional teams are the creators of tomorrow's competitive advantage.

Cross-functional teams represent all levels of an organization from different functional areas, including IT and often including business partners, suppliers, consultants, and customers—all working together toward a common goal.

The team assignment may call for different project management skills and methodologies. Led by an experienced project manager or owner, the discussions are not about subjective opinions or antidotal evidence but information, data, and project goals. No PowerPoint presentations or slideshows.

They start with questions and analysis of the available data and then use team-based wisdom to discover opinions, solutions, and ideas. The proposals and suggestions should be decomposed into the supporting arguments—the why and the how for each idea, which, in turn, will trigger more discoveries.

Cross-functional team leadership can be challenging. Project managers are responsible for overseeing team members with various ideas, opinions, and perspectives and then transforming those different variations of thought into a cohesive proposal.

Projects

Projects are unique, temporary, team-based endeavors with a series of initiatives designed to achieve a specific outcome. Projects may involve a single functional business unit, a cross-functional team, or joint venture with a business partner. They are frequently disbanded when the project is complete.

Developing a software application, creating a new product or service, implementing an organizational change, constructing a new building, and prototyping a new idea are all examples of projects.

Adaptive versus Predictive Projects

Agile or adaptive project methodologies are designed to be creative, with flexible goals that may change throughout the process. As the project team, along with its customer, plan, test, and learn, the requirements and specifications may change, which may alter the final deliverable. Continuous collaboration between the team's customer and the project team is the key to making fully informed decisions.

Waterfall or predictive project methodologies involve extensive planning, clearly defined goals, and a set timeline. The team works through specific steps in sequence, completing each level before moving on to the next one in the process. It is difficult to adapt to project changes or modifications or correct earlier steps. Given the incremental nature of adaptive planning, the result may differ from the original intent.

When evaluating which of the two approaches to take, consider whether the project has a predictable path or is a new frontier with an uncertain outcome.

Project Management

Successful project managers are skilled communicators with a proven ability to plan, organize, lead, and successfully complete the work of a project team, to achieve the project goals on time and within budget.

As you might expect, proven project managers are in high demand. Look for candidates with a tolerance for ambiguity who work well under pressure and are comfortable with change and complexity.

Good project managers can find the vital few out of the trivial many. They can see the big picture while understanding the small but crucial details. They have a calm temperament and a can-do, problem-solving attitude.

Meeting Facilitation

A facilitated meeting and a project-managed meeting have some overlapping activities but different goals.

A facilitator's role is one of managing a meeting's process toward the achievement of a consensus decision that is not necessarily unanimous. Ideas will arise that the team members agree on, are willing to accept, and believe would be a workable approach.

On the other hand, a project manager's job is one of overseeing a team-based development framework to design and successfully implement a project.

With a skilled facilitator guiding a cross-functional team with different perspectives, experiences, and backgrounds, almost any idea, problem, or opportunity can be the subject of a facilitated meeting.

A well-trained meeting facilitator is intuitive, has excellent verbal skills, is good at collaboration and relationships, and has a diplomatic communication style.

Standing in front of the participants the facilitator makes introductory remarks about the sponsor and purpose of the meeting and then describes the facilitator's and participants' responsibilities and the meeting's ground rules.

- There is no hierarchy; everyone has a vote.
- Do not challenge ideas; ask only clarifying questions.
- Discover themes from many ideas and perspectives.

- The facilitator:
  - o   is not a participant;
  - o   is neutral on the issues;
  - o   keeps the group focused;
  - o   encourages everyone's participation;
  - o   records, clarifies, and confirms the ideas;
  - o   supervises voting; and
  - o   publishes the conclusions.

Advanced reading material and outside speakers can be helpful ways to introduce subjects and encourage discussions.

A facilitated meeting can give an organization a significant advantage by increasing its creativity, innovation, and problem-solving abilities.

CHAPTER 5

Invest in Intangible Assets

Rethink Quarterly Earnings

In the constant battle to overcome disruptive change, high-potential organizations are increasing their investment in intangible or conceptual assets. Intangible assets are strategic expenditures designed to create value over many years.

An organization's investments in human capital, artificial intelligence, digital transformation, cloud computing, innovation, creativity, and team-based structures that can respond to changing customer requirements are all examples of intangible expenditures. Organizations that are not investing in conceptual intangibles will increasingly become competitively disadvantaged.

Amazon continues to dominate the e-commerce market through investments in intangible assets. Online sales and revenues are growing faster than traditional brick-and-mortar retail chains.

The Accounting Dilemma

The SEC has given the Financial Accounting Standards Board the responsibility of setting accounting standards for public companies in the United States. The public disclosure of an organization's financial information is available through auditors' reports, which include income and cash flow statements, the balance sheet, and supporting footnotes.

The primary source of future value creation, revenues, and profits will be based on talent, technology, innovative ideas, and adaptive organizational structures. The Financial Accounting Standards Board's generally accepted accounting principles (GAAP) treat most intangible investments as regular operating expenses in the income statement, versus capitalizing and amortizing these expenditures as an asset on the balance sheet.

For example, today's dynamic, constantly evolving IT systems developments are often a combination of third-party software, internal development, cloud computing platforms, services, and architectures, but the accounting rules for intangible expenditures are not flexible.

As a result, the revenue statement has lost much of its relevance, and the public financial information used by investors, lenders, regulators, and employees does not accurately reflect the organization's long-term strategic vision and strategies.

Although generally accepted accounting principles are routinely under review and updated, they will continue to struggle with the accounting for intangibles.

Non-GAAP Financial Information

Non-GAAP financial information can be helpful for investors and analysts who believe that GAAP accounting for intangibles may not capture a company's value.

Companies commonly supplement their reported GAAP earnings with non-GAAP financial information that they believe is a more accurate reflection of their results of operations or financial position.

Non-GAAP financial information is used by companies to bridge the divide between corporate reporting that is standardized under GAAP and a report tailored to their unique industries or circumstances. The SEC permits companies to present non-GAAP financial information in their public disclosures as well as registration statements if it complies with regulation G.

Staying Private—Nonvoting Stock

The number of US publicly held companies has fallen by 50 percent since the 1990s, partly due to firms staying private longer.

Some organizations are considering a dual-class initial public offering of nonvoting stock. Historically, these structures have been favored by family-owned companies seeking to preserve control. Nonvoting stock allows management to make operational decisions without influence from outside shareholders who may seek short-term gains at the expense of the organization's long-term strategic vision. Without legal intervention, the nonvoting stock typically trades at a discount.

Long-Term Stock Exchange

The long-term stock exchange will encourage organizational long-term strategic thinking. A primary feature of the long-term stock exchange is the idea of tenure voting. Where investors share voting power grows over time, capped at ten times the power of ordinary common stock after a decade.

A long-term stock exchange would result in new approaches to corporate governance and financial incentives and would need approval and compliance by the Securities and Exchange Commission.

CHAPTER 6

Experimentation, Prototyping, and Discovery

Giving up Control to Get Results

Disruptive change is forcing organizations to rethink longstanding business concepts. Historically, strategic planning was a senior management function that involved the identification of corporate goals and objectives. The planning process defined the business model and organizational structures, formulated strategies and actions, and was the basis for resource allocation and budgeting.

In the past, the strategic planning assumptions were based on the management's experience, knowledge, and judgment along with the organization's strengths, weaknesses, and the competitive position in the marketplace.

In today's environment of disruptive change, an assumption based on multiyear strategic planning is no longer a useful tool to direct and guide the organization's growth and long-term survival. In fact, strategic planning is dead; organizations cannot plan for an unknowable future.

Framed by a complex mixture of new, innovative technologies, changing demographics, and increasing consumer options, the question is how to design a new business model, one that can adapt to disruptive change. Moreover, one that meets the changing demands of today's customers and workforces. With a goal of adaptability and guided by the shared strategic vision, the new business model should organize as a team-based business structure designed for speed, agility, and innovation.

The old bureaucratic hierarchically structures that were designed to ensure predictability, conformity, and budget control are being replaced by a horizontal network of business units, functional workgroups, and cross-functional project teams collaborating through culture.

When freed from top-down, command and control decision-making, empowered employee teams can offer new forms of innovative thinking, problem-solving, products, services, and customer engagement strategies.

This hybrid flat and team-based structure can offer many significant advantages: both a horizontal and a vertical organizational structure; both functional and project-based; fewer traditional managers; more project managers; fluid boundaries and collaboration.

Cross-functional planning teams work together to experiment, prototype, and discover new innovative customer solutions.

Appoint a Chief Project Management Officer— Create a Project Management Culture

Reporting to the CEO and working with the leadership team, the chief project management officer has the following responsibilities:

- the analysis of the organization's strengths, weaknesses, opportunities, and threats
- monitoring relevant environmental and competitive trends
- facilitator and project management training
- assigning facilitators, project managers, and project team members

- the identification, prioritization, and recommendations for potential strategic initiatives
- management of project-based experimentation, prototyping, discovery, and learning
- educating teams on application program interface (API) gateways, application development kits, microservices, mobile app development platforms
- analysis and documentation of successes and failures
- scaling up and implementation of successful strategic initiatives

From Budgeting to Revenue-Based Income Statements

No matter the nature of the products or services the organization offers, the prices charged must cover your costs and support a reasonable profit.

A revenue-based income statement is a new method of continuous budget management where revenues generated from the organization's sales and services are allocated back to the business functions and project teams, based upon unit cost accounting and pricing assumptions. Think of this as reverse engineering—decomposing and redistributing the organization's revenue stream, based upon product and service cost assumptions, into a series of incomes statements.

Managing costs through functional revenue-based income statements are based on the fundamental tenets of pricing:

- ✓ Cover direct, indirect, overhead, and project costs.
- ✓ Be profitable.

Everyone is on the same page. There can be no stronger motivation for employees than openness and transparency. Sharing how we are doing as an organization and as a team, and the role we play in delivering the customer experience matters.

CHAPTER 7

Winning the Talent War

Eagles Do Not Flock; You Must Find Them One at a Time

Crafting and delivering a superior customer experience requires organizations to become employee centric. Organizations have long emphasized the customer value proposition—getting and keeping customers by exceeding their expectations profitably. They know that customers expect you to understand and cater to their unique likes, needs, wants, and preferences with every interaction. They measure consumer attitudes, product and brand preferences, media consumption habits, demographic and lifestyle characteristics. Organizations use artificial intelligence to gain personalized insights to deliver seamless and intuitive customer experiences.

In today's digital marketplace, where consumers have more control and choices, social media can make or break a brand's reputation.

Many of the customer branding and marketing concepts apply as well to winning the talent war. Like customers, talent is in demand. Like customers, talent has choices. Like customers, you do not pick talent; they pick you. Like customers, talent shops online for jobs. Customers check ratings; talent checks reputations. Customers check prices; talent checks salaries. Talented candidates are also customers.

On LinkedIn's "Most In-Demand Employers" and Glassdoor's "Best Places to Work," employees and former employees anonymously review companies and their management. An organization's reputation as an employer is public information. Candidates have access to employment search engines like Google for Jobs, Indeed, and Monster, which aggregate job listings websites, job boards, staffing firms, associations, and company career pages. Linkup only posts jobs offered on company websites, providing applicants with often unadvertised jobs.

The editors of Fast Company's magazine have sourced the globe to find enterprises at the forefront of their industries. With the breadth of innovation expanding, their 2018 Most Innovative Companies designation will reflect today's expanding innovation efforts across the business landscape.

It has become a candidates' marketplace.

The Workforce Challenges Ahead for Business

Businesses are discussing how to organize and innovate to attract, recruit, develop, keep, manage, and engage the twenty-first-century workforce. They're redesigning the organization for speed, agility, and adaptability. The new adaptive business models are changing how work is done and will need new skills, knowledge, and competencies along with a new approach to leadership development— more digital, younger, team oriented with project management skills.

The traditional transaction-based HR department is not prepared to handle the workforce talent management challenges.

Appoint a Chief Talent Officer

A complex and evolving position, the chief talent officer (CTO) will play a critical role in the organization's future. With responsibility for creating the organization's talent management strategies and building a strong employer brand and career website, the ideal candidate must have the ability to understand the changing talent management market dynamics and translate them into actionable strategies through proven leadership and communication skills.

If possible, appoint a CTO from within the organization talent pool who understands the organizational culture and supports the shared strategic vision statement.

Reporting to the CEO and partnering with the chief marketing officer, chief artificial intelligence officer, and select recruiting firms, the CTO is responsible for the design, implementation, and success of the organization's talent management strategies, including the following:

- employee value proposition
- employer branding/career website
- pre-hire assessment

- talent acquisition/employee referrals
- onboarding/engagement/retention can't
- talent management/career development
- performance management
- coaching and mentoring
- workforce/succession planning
- culture/employee experience

Aging Multigenerational Workforce

Ten thousand baby boomers are turning sixty-five every day. One of the most significant workforce issues organizations face is the loss of leadership and skills from retirements, a trend that is projected to continue through 2029.

Generation X is an important pool of organizational talent and leadership, but they do not have the numbers to fill the skills gap created by the retiring baby boomers. The millennial generation, born between 1980and 2000, is the largest in history, significantly larger than the baby boomers and reported to control $24 trillion of wealth by 2020. Highly educated and technically competent, with an entrepreneurial mind-set, millennials want to be coached and mentored, not managed. They care more about social issues, organizational culture, growth potential, and work-life balance than prior generations. They view nine-to-five regular office hours as a thing of the past, question conventional wisdom, and do not want to be stuck in organizational status quo with companies that resist change and new ideas. They prefer a collaborative and innovative, team-oriented environment with group decisions. They expect the organization to offer them development opportunities to learn, grow, and expand their knowledge and skills when seeking out new jobs or deciding to stay.

Millennials use social media to connect to brands and services. They are willing to share information online about their brand preferences. Once they lose faith in a brand, it is very difficult to win them back.

Generation Z or the internet generation, born 2000 and after, has never known a world without technology. Computers and smartphones influence their social communications, work styles, and motivations. Many self-identify as digital device addicts.

In our digital world, generation Z processes information faster, switches between work and play faster, and has more experience at multitasking than prior generations.

They make up 25 percent of the US population, making them a broader demographic group than the baby boomers or millennials. As they enter the workforce, digital technology will be an important aspect of their careers.

The Gig Economy, Strategic Alliances, and Startups

In today's digital age, the workforce is mobile; you can work anywhere, so the location and jobs are more independent, separated, and uncoupled. Welcome to the gig economy, where workers are part-time, temps, short-term, freelancing, and self-employed contractors.

Forming mutually beneficial relationships with strategic business partners has several advantages. In today's environment, it is impossible for any organization to have all the specialized technical skills and knowledge that are necessary to compete and prosper. Properly selected strategic alliances can match what you are good at with what your partners are good at.

Create a Startup Department

Hire entrepreneurial millennials and create a startup department to deliver new or variations on existing products and services for the current and future customers. Small autonomous startups with cross-functional teams—testing, experimenting, prototyping, and discovery—are the future.

The Challenges

The CTO and the talent management team face multiple challenges, including the following:

- workforce and succession planning
- transferring the critical skills, knowledge, and expertise from the older retiring workforce to the younger employees who think differently, have different values and expectations
- creating a positive employee experience and employer reputation
- applying the principles of marketing to employer branding and career websites
- attracting, developing, and keeping top talent

Recruiting Adaptive Leaders

First, assume that disruptive change will accelerate, not subside. Recruit, develop, and promote change agents, problem-solvers, and future leaders for their natural competencies and potential rather than academic intelligence and pedigree. Look for tolerance for ambiguity, the ability to find the vital few out of the trivial many, and an understanding that mistakes within reason are expected.

Recruiting potential leaders in an age of exponential change will be challenging. Everything is evolving; our understanding, thinking, and opinions may be retrospective and not current, and our prior experience less relevant. Historically, employees adapted to their managers and the organization. In the future, to attract and keep talent, management and leadership must adapt to the employees. However, recruiting transformational leadership talent is essential to the organization's long-term survival.

We define natural competencies and potential as the behavioral patterns, personality traits, and individual attributes and abilities that form the foundation for how well the leader can align people and teams with the shared strategic vision and the goal of becoming an adaptive organization.

Matching Task and Talent

Assessing Natural Competencies and Potential

The big five personality factors'—extroversion, agreeableness, conscientiousness, emotional stability, and openness—influence on workplace behavior has been evaluated in many studies with large numbers of people and has been widely used for classifying social and emotional learning skills.

We prefer NeuroColor's personality assessment because it was started with biology and has had the results confirmed by biology. NeuroColor uses the neuroscience behind our personality to provide a new perspective on some of the most significant challenges facing organizations, including hiring, personnel development, employee engagement, high-performance teambuilding, innovation, and customer insights. The system can leverage personality inside the workplace in ways never possible before.

Dr. Helen Fisher, biological anthropologist and cofounder of NeuroColor, studied numerous aspects in biological literature, including genetics, disease, gender, drug, and twin research. She discovered that many measurable personality traits fall into four broad styles of thinking and behavior associated with the four broad brain systems based on dopamine, serotonin, testosterone, and estrogen.

Fisher developed a personality questionnaire based on her discovery, then used extensive statistical analysis and functional magnetic resonance imaging (fMRI) to the brain to confirm her theory. Over fourteen million people in forty countries have taken her personality inventory, and her peer-reviewed and duplicated research results have been published in top scientific journals.

At NeuroColor, Dr. Fisher and cofounder David Labno have developed and validated a business-focused second-generation questionnaire. The NeuroColor Temperament Inventory questionnaire measures the degree to which a person expresses personality traits in each of the four broad brain systems. The questionnaire offers a series of statements to which the user indicates the level of agreement. As part of the personality report, NeuroColor provides a graph illustrating how strongly the user responses agree with the characteristics of each neural system. The NeuroColor personality report uses this information to makes specific recommendations to improve effectiveness, including how the user communicates and interacts with others.

NeuroColor communicates through color to help make the concepts behind the tool easier to understand as well as more memorable. The NeuroColor personality report uses four colors: red, yellow, green, and blue. The user's intensity (0 percent to 100 percent) represents the intensity of each of the four broad brain systems that contribute to personality.

Yellow is the dopamine system. People who express certain genes in the dopamine system tend to be curious, creative, spontaneous, energetic, and mentally flexible. They are risk-takers and seek novelty. They are good at brainstorming and trying new things. They are bored with routine and alienated by rules and structure.

Green represents the estrogen system. People who are expressive of the estrogen/oxytocin system tend to be intuitive, introspective, imaginative, trusting, empathetic, and idealistic. They are sensitive to people's feelings and typically have good verbal and social skills. They are good at collaboration and relationships, and they are diplomatic but dislike politics, conflict, and inflexibility.

Red stands for the testosterone system. People expressive of the testosterone system are tough-minded, direct, decisive, skeptical, assertive, emotionally contained, inventive, experimental, analytical, and competitive. They tend to be good at engineering, computers, mechanics, and math but feel alienated by indecision, lack of focus, and inefficiency.

Blue is the serotonin system. People who have high serotonin activity are eager to belong and prefer familiar friends and workplaces. They are traditional in their values and less inclined toward exploration. They are calm, cooperative, cautious, persistent, detail oriented, facts oriented, and structured. Being good at detailed planning, they are organized and consistent but dislike disorder, ambiguity, and uncertainty.

The four broad brain systems that contribute to our personalities play a large role in determining how we think and behave, but the brain systems are not mutually exclusive. If an individual is high in yellow, that does not mean they lack blue, green, or red. We are a composite of the four brain systems, although most of our behaviors and thinking are aligned with one or two. When evaluating yourself and others, consider all four biological systems. When you understand where someone lands on each scale, you begin to see the full personality.

Position Descriptions

Today's chief talent officers understand the importance of well-written position descriptions for recruiting, selection, hiring, development, promotions, and succession planning. Traditional job descriptions are not effective because they fail to define the nature of the position requirements fully. Today's position descriptions expand on the job functions, skills, knowledge, and technical experience with behavioral patterns, personality traits, and individual attributes necessary for success in each position.

The combined power of NeuroColor's Personality Assessment and the position-based talent management programs can create a highly effective match of task and talent.

Diversity of Minds

Disruptive change is prompting significant shifts in corporate paradigms and management strategies. Organizations are moving from a top-down vertical structure to a horizontal, team-based approach. Nontraditional thinking is changing the world. Historically, we expect the relationship between the past and the future to be linear, but in today's world, our choices based on that way of thinking are often proven wrong.

Increase a team's effectiveness by increasing the diversity of minds, personality traits, and perspectives. A cross-functional team can find patterns and explore aspects from many angles, which helps them think differently and creatively. The dynamics of teamwork are more important than the talents of the individuals who make up the team.

Change is always difficult. Digital transformation, artificial intelligence, and the seamless engagement of the changing customer demands are reshaping the company's talent management programs. The right people, in the right jobs, are the critical differentiators of success.

The NeuroColor Personality Assessment can help the organization's leaders, teams, and individuals become more effective.

Artificial Intelligence—Matching People to Jobs

Predictive algorithms, cognitive computing, and machine learning are rapidly emerging as essential tools to help organizations find the best candidates. AI's strength is its ability to analyze huge quantities of data, look across variables, and find insights and patterns that humans might never find.

Organizations are increasingly using AI to find whether there is a good match between the position description and the combination of the applicant's resume and the public information available on the web. Also, AI can help decide if the applicant is a good fit for the organization's culture and likely to stay with the organization for a significant time.

IBM's Personality Insights service is based on the psychology of language combined with a data analytics algorithm to discover actionable insights about people and entities. Google's Cloud Job Discovery uses machine learning to better understand both job content and the intent of job seekers. Artificial intelligence tends to be used in the early stages of the process when organizations are narrowing down the pool of candidates.

Corporate Culture and the Employee Value Proposition

Workforce job satisfaction and retention directly correlate with the organization's culture—values, beliefs, and attitudes that characterize the organization and guide its practices, the way decisions are made, and how management responds to threats and opportunities.

Culture starts at the top with leadership doing the following:

- formulating, communicating, and living a shared strategic vision for the future
- communicating the importance of adapting to disruptive change and being willing to rethink the organizational structures and the decision-making processes
- prioritizing the employee experience—coaching, mentoring, and personal development
- recruiting and keeping highly sought-after talent
- onboarding, socializing, and engaging new employees

Employer Branding and the Employee Experience

Branding and marketing are about using words and phrases to persuade and motivate the audience. They are about convincing a prospect that you understand their needs and have something of value to offer.

The employee experience, and thus retention, is often based on cultural fit, the technological tools to collaborate, and if their unique requirements are being considered, discussed, and addressed.

Before you begin writing your story, do your homework. Understand your audience. Gather knowledge and perspectives by applying traditional customer marketing techniques. Group existing employees into segments based upon age, demographics, and the employment lifecycle. Consider using focus groups, surveys, and interviews to understand workforce attitudes, opinions, and requirements. Position the organization's employment story by asking and answering the following questions:

- Are millennials our target audience?
- How are we different from other employment opportunities?
- Why would candidates want to work here?

- What is the overlap with our customer branding copy?
- Should we write an employer branding tagline?

When writing copy, do not lose sight of the goals: selling the organization's employee brand and attracting the best talent. Be specific, be correct, be organized, and appeal to both the emotions and the intellect. Make the copy candidate-centered, with the candidate's interests in mind.

A good way to connect with prospective candidates is through testimonials—favorable workforce experiences, stories, and views from existing employees and customers.

A great employer branding tagline can make the benefits of employment with the organization clear to prospective talent. It can be difficult to succinctly express your employee story, so keep it simple, memorable, positive, and upbeat. In many ways, it is like writing a mini shared vision statement.

CHAPTER 8

Digital Transformation

Managing Digital Disruption

Digital transformation is a categorical imperative for long-term success and survival. The constant stream of new technologies is blurring industry boundaries and redefining markets, overrunning the ability of organizations to keep up. Facing radical change, business models, companies, and entire industries are at risk of digital disruption. Digital transformation demands the leadership's attention, understanding, and action.

It Cannot Be Delegated. It Must Be Led.

It may be an uncomfortable subject for many executives but an unavoidable obligation. With an investment of time and some coaching, the terminology, concepts, and principles are understandable.

The House That Jack Built

As in the construction industry, the presence of an existing structure that needs extensive renovations will increase the complexity of new systems development and can be daunting.

In many organizations, the older legacy computer systems and programming languages may still be functioning. Like the house that Jack built, legacy systems have been patched, repatched, and modified many times. Some stairways lead nowhere, and doors open into blank walls.

Legacy systems, designed for effectiveness and efficiency, are inflexible and hard to support or expand. Frequently, the original development staff has changed assignments, retired, or left the organization. It is not uncommon that these systems are poorly documented and difficult, if not impossible, to integrate with newer systems development projects.

However, in today's digital world, organizations must be nimble and able to change direction quickly. They must innovate, experiment, learn, and adapt, creating new products and services that satisfy the customers' changing needs faster than the competition.

The forces of digital disruption are:

- smarter devices
- exploding cloud services
- third-party software vendors
- microservices and application program interface (API) application development
- 5G fifth generation wireless networks

It requires organizations to reinvent themselves, think differently, and rethink everything. Digital transformation is about the twenty-first-century digital business organization. Although challenging, investment in digital transformation will reward those who are successful and punish the status quo.

Questions for Leadership and the Board of Directors

- Does the board of directors have the digital ability for a meaningful conversation with the leadership team on digital transformation?
- Have we spent the time to discuss and understand the technological changes we are facing?
  - The opportunities and risks of digital disruption and technology-based innovation?
  - Are we making digital transformation decisions with outdated information and perspectives?
  - Have we aligned our digital transformation strategy team with our development and business management operation teams?
  - Are we at risk of digital disruption from within or outside of our industry?
  - Are we studying the best practices of the digital giants for application to our business?
  - Have we identified and prioritized possible digital disruptive impacts to our business model and organization?
  - Are we discussing the possible secondary side effects of digital disruption on our organization?
  - If we fall behind our competitors' digital initiatives, will we be able to catch up?

- What is our level of risk tolerance?
  - o Are we willing to innovate, prototype, experiment, and accept failures?
  - o To create new opportunities, are we actively seeking the possibility of willful self-disruption?
- Are we versatile?
  - o Can we manage today's business functions while we actively explore digital ideas to replace those functions?
  - o Do we have the diversity of talent and perspectives to make the problematic digital transformation choices?
  - o Do we have a cross-functional team-based collaborative work environment?
- Is project management one of the organization's core competencies?
- Do we have the courage and talent to act in the long-term best interests of the organization?

There is no road map or technical sequence to digital transformation. It is a continuing incremental journey, a nonlinear process of phased assimilation, learning, testing, and problem-solving, making new ideas part of our collective knowledge.

Digital transformation planning should begin with the assumption that technological change will continue to quicken and permeate every aspect of the enterprise.

The Internet of Things connectivity is designed into every electronically enabled product. Beyond keywords and phrases, search engines have added voice recognition and visual search abilities, resulting in redesigned websites. Blockchain technology, advances in machine learning, and artificial intelligence are becoming commonplace.

The leadership team, functional management, and the technology professionals must jointly develop an adaptive and disruption-resistant digital business strategy. Your digital business strategy and your digital transformation strategy are one subject.

The potential competitive advantage of the organization's digital strategy lies in the leadership's ability to conceptualize how technology can differentiate the organization's computing infrastructure and application development processes with the ability to innovate, experiment, and adapt quickly.

Change Is Not Optional—Innovation Not Voluntary

Managing an organization-wide digital transformation project requires a significant share of the organization's time and attention. The strategic importance of the planning calls for the organization's most successful project managers and change agents, with broad authority, willing to challenge conventional wisdom, praise, prod, and act. A weekly project meeting with the CEO and the leadership team can improve the odds of success.

How do you approach digital transformation?
You cannot look to the past for what has worked.
You cannot trust your instincts because everything is changing.
Whom do you ask?
Whom do you listen to?

Get Help

No organization has all the talents, skills, and proficiencies necessary for digital transformation. Information technology research firms like International Data Corporation

(IDC), Gartner, Inc., and Forrester can give helpful insights into digital transformation, cloud computing, and vendor choice.

Build a Digital Transformation (DX) Team

First, assign the leadership team's executive champion and the project manager. Then select a large multidisciplined cross-functional team from IT, business operations, finance, marketing, sales, and legal.

The goal is to design a sustainable, disruption-resistant digital transformation business strategy. The DX team cannot propose solutions without broadly understanding the new technological alternatives available—their advantages, benefits, disadvantages, and risks. For example, cloud computing is a set of vendor services, not computing hardware.

Digital transformation also requires a thorough understanding of the organization's current and future business requirements:

- customer requirements—services and functionality
- security, trust, backup and recovery

- innovative app development—microservices
- legal/regulatory requirements
- competitor initiatives within and outside the industry

Because of the extent of the subject matter and the need for creativity and open discussions, each DX team members should be assigned several subject discussion groups.

A Digital Business Journey

Although vendors and experts do not always agree with IT terminology, let us begin our guided digital transformation journey with some concepts. The transition from traditional IT infrastructure to a hybrid cloud is a process that requires an understanding of the different cloud models.

Infrastructure

Infrastructure is the set of technologies that are the foundation for the operations and management of the organization's IT services—the combination of computing and networking hardware, data storage, servers, backup and firewall security, and management software to optimize the workload.

There are four types of infrastructure:

- traditional
- converged
- hyperconverged
- composable

Traditional infrastructure is a data center architecture that runs the workloads using different kinds of hardware—computing, storage, networking, and servers. The advantage is that it is in your data center, and it can be cost-effective and reliable if supported by a well-trained staff. The disadvantage is that it creates different physical hardware silos that operations management tools cannot cross. The result is a static environment that is rigid, cumbersome to deploy, and involves varying degrees of human intervention with specialized teams.

Converged infrastructure brings together for a given workload the four components of a data center—computing, storage, networking, and server virtualization—into a single operating platform. This approach can help lessen the complexity of a traditional data center and position the use of a unique integrated cloud computing environment, but it does not give the flexibility to alter the configuration.

Hyperconverged infrastructure is an operating environment that shares computing and storage resources through software-defined storage, software-defined computing, and commoditized hardware with a unitized management interface. The primary difference is that with hyperconverged infrastructure, the network and the underlying storage abstractions are implemented virtually in software rather than physically in hardware.

Neither converged nor hyperconverged offer a single operating platform for all workloads.

Composable infrastructure—infrastructure as code. It is a fully integrated environment, software-defined, single operating platform that brings together a fluid pool of computing, storage, and network resources. Composability is a systems design principle that deals with the interrelationships of components. A composable infrastructure is built from a collection of modular components that can be configured and reconfigured to meet the workload requirements. Build a sustainable, innovation-based, competitive advantage with a composable infrastructure.

Cloud Computing Services

Cloud computing is an information technology system for enabling ubiquitous access to shared pools of configurable resources, networks, servers, storage, applications, and services, which can be provisioned rapidly with minimal management effort or service provider interaction.

Cloud computing has on-demand self-service, broad network access, and resource pooling.

It is scalable with rapid elasticity or expansion and with measured services.

Cloud computing delivers computing services over a virtual private network or through the internet where the services are available anywhere, anytime, and with any device or browser. The service is elastic and scalable, dynamically allocating additional resources as needed. Moreover, cloud computing services typically use a pay-as-you-go model. The availability of high-capacity networks, low-cost computers, and storage devices as well as the widespread adoption of hardware visualization, service-oriented architecture, and utility-based computing has led to the growth of cloud computing.

Cloud computing offers an opportunity to minimize up-front IT infrastructure costs. As well, third-party clouds enable organizations to focus on getting their applications up and running faster instead of using resources on computer infrastructure.

The transition from a traditional IT computing infrastructure to a cloud based IT is an incremental process. Cloud computing is not limited to a multitenant public cloud hosted in a vendor's data center. It is also about single tenant private clouds hosted in the corporate data center or a vendor's facilities. In many situations, the optimal solution is a hybrid combination of these choices.

Cloud Delivery Models: Public Cloud, Private Cloud, Community Cloud, Hybrid Cloud

Public cloud infrastructure is designed for use by the general public. Public clouds represent the outsourcing of computing resources or software applications to a multitenant computer hosted on the premises of the cloud provider. IBM's BlueMix, Microsoft's Azure, and Amazon Web Services are examples of public cloud computing. Public cloud customers are essentially renting an on-demand computing utility service on a fine-grained pay-as-you-go basis. The resources are available over the internet using a web browser or through a virtual private network connection. Some organizations use public cloud storage services for backup instead of buying the more costly on-premises physical storage software and devices.

For customers, the public cloud delivery models convert traditional IT capital expenditures into operational expenditures, thus lowering the barrier to entry. Public cloud users need not pay for the resources and equipment to meet their peak workload demands. By design, public clouds are multitenant, meaning that your applications and data are virtually petition and isolated but still running on the same computer with other public cloud customers. You may have noisy neighbors, longer response times, and higher security risks.

Consider the public cloud model:

- easy to access and use
- security of data and application
- heavy workload of apps with many users
- project collaboration
- testing and development

- on-demand with unlimited scalability
- software as a service provider in place
- no need to invest in infrastructure, maintenance, software, and updates

Private cloud is a single-tenant cloud infrastructure model, provisioned for the exclusive use of an organization made up of multiple customers or a business unit. It may be owned, managed, and operated by the organization, a third party, or some combination and may exist on or off premises.

Private cloud infrastructures can offer most of the features provided by the public cloud but safely behind the organization's firewall and within its private network. Private clouds give greater control, security, and performance.

As with the public cloud, if users deploy applications calling for growth, the private cloud is easily scalable if the underlying resource hardware pools are available. An organization's IT department can build a private cloud within their own data centers or use infrastructure as a service (IaaS) tools of a private cloud vendor.

Consider the private cloud model:

- secures business's critical data and apps
- strict security and data privacy
- assures compliance with governmental regulations
- keeps private data private
- fewer concerns about public cloud reliability

The community cloud is a multitenant cloud infrastructure provisioned for the exclusive use by a specific community of customers from organizations that share interests, missions, security requirements, and compliance considerations. It may be managed and operated by one or more of the organizations, by a third party, or some combination. Moreover, it can be on or off premises.

The hybrid cloud is often the best solution. The hybrid cloud computing architecture is a combination of two or more different cloud infrastructures (i.e., private, community, or public). Each remains a unique entity, but they are brought together by proprietary technology that enables data and application to work together cohesively.

The business-critical data and applications are typically hosted in the private cloud, safely behind the company firewall, while the public cloud usually hosts the less critical business applications and data.

When computing and processing demand rises and falls, hybrid cloud computing gives businesses the ability to seamlessly scale their on-premises infrastructure up to the public cloud to handle any overflow, without providing third-party vendor data centers access to the entirety of their data.

The hybrid cloud infrastructure provides the organization's IT development team with the ability to build, test, and deploy applications in the public cloud environment while supporting and protecting the on-premises production operating environment assets.

Internal employees can use the organization's intranet to access the private cloud for applications and processes. The website, prospects, customers, salesforce, and distributed employees use the internet to access the organization's public cloud, which in turn has a virtual private network connection to the enterprise's public cloud.

Security systems provide user identity and access management for on-premises, cloud, and mobile app endpoints. The users do not need to consider whether the application is running in the cloud or on premises.

Using a hybrid cloud not only allows companies to scale computing resources, but it also removes the need for computing hardware to handle short-term spikes in demand.

Organizations sometimes pay a private cloud vendor for temporary resources instead of buying and supporting more equipment that could remain idle over long periods of time.

Hybrid clouds can present some technical challenges. Private cloud workloads must access and interact with public cloud providers that need an application program interface (API) compatibility and virtual private network connectivity.

Hybrid cloud computing model can be the best of all worlds. It is a platform that delivers flexibility, scalability, and cost efficiencies, with the lowest possible risk of data exposure.

Consider the hybrid cloud model:

- security being paramount, multiple secure platforms

- can send noncritical workloads to the public cloud
  - o load balancing between clouds
- require software as a service security
- unique requirements for different databases
- different support requirements for
  - o customers
  - o internal departments and employees
  - o business partners and suppliers

Three Cloud Services

Infrastructure as a Service

Infrastructure as a Service (IaaS) creates the fundamental building blocks for cloud services. IaaS is highly automated and scalable, with user provisioning of computing, storage, and network capabilities. Organizations can build a virtual data center in the cloud with on-demand access to many of the same technologies and resources of a traditional data center, without the significant investments associated with planning, maintenance, and management. It is accessed through the internet or on a virtual private network with a static IP address.

Some providers offer infrastructure as a service, with their unique value propositions and service portfolios. Cloud providers typically bill IaaS services on a utility computing basis; cost reflects the number of resources allocated and consumed.

Platform as a Service

Platform as a Service and application platform as a service are both development and deployment frameworks in the cloud. The platform as a service offers customer development teams an opportunity to deliver everything from web-based applications, a single cloud-based application, or sophisticated cloud-enabled business applications. The platform can provide database management tools for artificial intelligence, business analytics, finding insights and patterns, machine learning, and forecasting.

As with infrastructure as a service, platforms as a service includes infrastructure—computing, networking, storage, and servers. Providers typically bill IaaS services on a utility computing basis; cost reflects the number of resources allocated and consumed.

Software as a Service

Software as a Service (SaaS) moves the management of software and development to a third-party service. SaaS is a licensing and delivery model for software that is licensed on a subscriber basis and hosted centrally. The SaaS capability reduces the expense of software ownership by eliminating the need for technical staff to install and upgrade the purchased software. The software provider's applications run on a third-party cloud infrastructure and are accessible from various client devices.

Software as a service could be described as third-party, commercial, or on-demand software and has become a typical delivery model for many business software applications, including the following:

- email, messaging, and collaboration
- payroll processing
- document management
- computer-aided design
- accounting and invoicing
- customer relationship management
- enterprise resource planning
- human resource management and talent acquisition
- content management

Cloud Vendor Selection

Some organizations are looking to the cloud as the best long-term approach to digital transformation. Using cloud services allows a focus on customers, shareholders, and employees. However, selecting the right cloud vendor is essential.

Consider cloud providers that:

- display a deep commitment to all three layers of the cloud
  - o IaaS—infrastructure as a service
  - o PaaS—platform as a service
  - o SaaS—software as a service
- actively support artificial intelligence and machine learning
- can help convert legacy systems to the cloud
- offer permissioned blockchain technology

However, there are considerations in the choice of vendors. The cloud vendor services can be proprietary and not interoperable. Moving from one cloud vendor to another may be difficult. It can involve data alteration with substantial migration costs. Some customers opt to stay with their current cloud provider, even if they are not meeting their requirements. Some have termed this concept *vendor lock-in.*

No matter which cloud vendors are selected or which infrastructure deployment model is chosen, it is imperative that the organization keep control over data security.

Digital Transformation—Cloud Computing

Unlike traditional approaches to information technology, cloud computing focus is on services, not hardware. Cloud computing is a paradigm shift, a fundamental change in the underlying approach to information technology management and control. Today's cloud computing offers customer access to shared pools of configurable system resources and software applications that can be quickly provisioned with minimal management effort.

As business becomes increasingly digitally connected, cloud computing enables on-demand network access to shared pools of configurable computing resources, connecting any device, anytime and anywhere, driving every business strategy. As the foundation for innovation and digital transformation, the cloud has become the de facto model for computing services, providing previously unattainable scalability and cost-effectiveness.

Today, there are more cloud service providers, more infrastructures, more services, along with the evolution of single cloud data centers to a multicloud environment. Cloud services have fundamentally reshaped business practices along with the functions, responsibilities, and the required skills of information technology organizations.

Cloud computing services have increased at a compound growth rate of about 20 percent per annum. In that same period, traditional data center spending is down by 40 percent, while public cloud and private cloud spending are growing. Platform as a service spending has grown by 50 percent, and cloud system infrastructure as a service spending has increased over 200 percent.

Software as a service deployment is predicted to be 60 percent of all cloud-based workloads. Most organizations run software as a service across multiple cloud vendors. For example, payroll, human resources, financial, customer, and marketing services' software applications could be implemented with different vendor clouds. For unique applications and highly customized cloud solutions, Amazon, Microsoft, and IBM are the vendors of choice.

To manage data security and privacy risks, about half of today's organizations run their critical applications and data workloads on private clouds, provisioned exclusively for their organization. The private cloud infrastructure may be owned, managed, and operated by the organization, by a third party, or by some combination and may exist on or off premises.

Hybrid cloud infrastructure is a multicloud combination of two or more distinct cloud infrastructures (private, community, or public) that remain a unique entity and are brought together by proprietary technology that enables data and application portability between clouds.

Consumer expectations are for highly responsive, fast-loading services and applications, but today's 4G (fourth generation) wireless communications is becoming overloaded, producing latency, propagation delays, increased response times, and reduced throughput in addition to the cybersecurity risks.

A Digitally Transformed Economy

The Overload Challenge

- a Gartner forecast that by 2020 over twenty billion devices will be connected to the internet
- from the internet of people to the internet of everything
    - sensors embedded in transportation, buildings, health care, wearables, communications, and utilities
- visual search platforms with image downloads
- growing demand for internet video streaming services—Netflix
- text messaging, voice and video calls, images, media, and documents
- a forecast that by 2022, over 70 percent of software interactions in an organization will be on mobile devices, smartphones, tablets, and wearables
- API gateways/application development kits, microservices, and mobile app development platforms making it easy for both developers and employees to create, publish, maintain, monitor, and secure mobile applications
    - the layers of complexity in cloud computing services being abstracted away, creating

a level of simplicity so people can interact
with today's technology

- virtual assistants, distributed artificial intelligence, and machine learning—moving to the edge of the internet
- personalized digital marketing
- processor chip design flaws requiring operating system patches
- cloud computing scalability and flexibility
- augmented and virtual reality
- backup and recovery services—more granular, more frequent, faster recovery
- end-to-end security technologies
  - biometrics-based identification and access management, hosted in the cloud
  - military-level encryption and decryption
  - managed cybersecurity services—MSSP
- blockchain technology—secure by design, a trusted transactional application
  - computationally demanding with high bandwidth

As with other technology decisions, cloud computing services have pros and cons, advantages and disadvantages, benefits and risks.

The Benefits of Cloud Computing Services

- fewer specialized IT staff needed
- less expensive—both up-front and operating
- access—any device, anytime, anywhere
- innovation, agility, and scalability
- disaster backup and recovery
- software as a service
  - customer relationship management—sales
  - billing, collection, and financials
  - human resources—payroll
  - email and office productivity
  - document management
  - social networks
- platform as a service
  - software development speed
  - artificial intelligence
  - business analytics

The Downside of Cloud Computing Services

- latency—time-critical applications
- employee device security
- downtime—network availability
- compliance management
- public cloud—security risks
- vendor lock-in

CHAPTER 9

Virtual Organizations

Unified Communications as a Service

As the enterprise's digital future becomes increasingly based on cloud services, a new form of organizational communications, a virtual organization, is evolving. In pursuit of an adaptive vision, a virtual organization can distribute work and workers as well as reshape communications and collaboration with customers, suppliers, business partners, departments, and project team members, working together in real time, sharing ideas, satisfying customers, and co-creating new products and services.

Virtual organizations are cloud-based unified communications and collaboration services designed uniquely for each organization, with a single administrator, centralized membership authorization, scalable cloud computing, and storage.

Historically, organizations would acquire and install their own communications infrastructure. The combination of cloud services, voiceover IP, software-defined networks, and data centers has created a cloud-based software-defined communications infrastructure.

Description—Unified Communications as a Service

- video, voice, and telephony
- messaging—email, voicemail, and unified messaging
- conferencing—multiparty audio, video, and web
- share and manage files, documents, and applications
- instant messaging and presence
    - o send information to individuals or groups
    - o see the status of individuals
- offering multiple communication functions
    - o mobile devices, smartphones, tablets, thin browser clients, and desktop clients
    - o specialized clients in business applications

- integrated communication applications
  - contact centers and communications platforms as a service
  - workstream collaboration—sharing knowledge, problem-solving, solutions, content, and communication in real time

Unified Communications as a Service Vendors

The UCaaS vendors focus on cloud delivery has accelerated as their offerings exceed the traditional on-premises communications capabilities. The UCaaS offerings are complex and evolving, and the landscape is fragmented, making vendor evaluation and selection even more challenging.

- communication service providers, CSPs
  - AT&T, Verizon, and others
  - core strengths—data and voice services
  - face challenges—new strategies
- technology vendors
  - Google, Amazon, IBM, and Microsoft
  - cloud service providers
- UCaaS specialists
  - RingCentral, Fuze, and 8X8
  - offer platforms and services

As with other cloud-based services, UCaaS can be hosted by the vendor, on-premises, or a hybrid of both. The hybrid solution gives organizations the flexibility to make a phased transition to a unified communications cloud service. The virtual organization can communicate from a portfolio of devices to unlock the collaborative power of groups and teams.

Becoming a virtual organization requires a visionary leader and a highly skilled implementation team for project planning and design. Much like a startup company, the project team should consider a minimally viable project approach. Select an area and use a prototyping concept for testing, learning, redesigning, rethinking, and retesting. Embrace team-based innovation, creativity, experimentation, prototyping, and discovery through a cloud-based unified digital communications service. It is an opportunity to increase productivity and deliver better products and services at a lower cost, as well as improve communications and collaboration between teams, departments, customers, external partners, and suppliers.

Digital transformation is no small feat, so think differently and rethink everything.

Out-collaborate the competition.

CHAPTER 10

Fifth-Generation Wireless Networks

Transforming Communications

The fifth generation wireless network will not only address the challenges of cybersecurity and the exponential growth of mobile devices; it will be transformative and potentially disruptive, creating new businesses and new industries, profoundly changing how many organizations work and how we live our lives. 5G is not an evolution of the current 4G wireless networks but instead a revolution in wireless communications technology.

The marketing term "5G" is used for the fifth-generation wireless communications network that will ensure end-to-end trust, security, and confidence. With global radio frequency spectrum harmonization, international governmental and private sector joint development, the fifth-generation digital network will deliver ultrahigh bandwidth, throughput, and imperceivable latency, the time a message takes to transverse the system. With highly mobile and highly connected density, the global deployment of new 5G services is expected to impact nearly every industry and job sector.

The first phases of precommercial testing of the new 5G technology standards are underway. Service providers like AT&T and Verizon are experimenting with 5G trials in California, Massachusetts, Georgia, Michigan, New Jersey, Texas, and Washington, DC. The UK is planning a small number of large-scale deployment pilots to find the practical and economic challenges of 5G mobile networks. They are expected to start pilot testing in 2018/19 with completion in 2019/20 or 2020/21. Experts don't anticipate commercial 5G until 2020 or later.

The 5G network and the new radio (NR) cellular air interface deployment are likely to be phased. For example, urban development could provide a platform for testing autonomous vehicles, traffic control, public safety, and security. In rural areas, 5G deployment pilots could test the connectivity of the internet of things services for remote healthcare and agriculture.

One operator plans to implement 5G in the urban areas first, with the rest of the network using the 4G backbone. As a result, the segments of the 5G network that operates on the higher frequencies will not be backward compatible.

The fifth generation communications network will be a sea change, supporting a large number of new industries, new services, and deployment models through a diverse set of devices with different latency and performance requirements.

The 5G Network Services

Ultralow latency is the service provider's chief technology challenge.

- **Ultra-Reliable and Low-Latency Communications Almost Instantaneous—1 ms Latency—uRLLC**
    o mission-critical services
        ▪ latency-sensitive services requiring extremely high reliability, availability, and security
    o connected cars traffic safety
    o robot control

- o   electricity grid control
- o   intelligent transportation systems
- o   cellular drone communications
- o   tactile internet applications
  - ▪ human real-time interacting with machines
    - • visual feedback
    - • controlled with an imperceptible time lag
      - o   one millisecond end-to-end latency
    - • virtual reality gloves
      - o   enables touch in virtual reality
  - ▪ telepresence
    - • remote inspection, maintenance, and repair
  - ▪ healthcare
    - • remote physical examination
    - • telesurgery
  - ▪ serious gaming
    - • health care, education, training, and simulation
- **Enhanced Mobile Broadband—eMBB**
  - o   the data-intensive high-capacity entertainment services
    - ▪ 4k/8k video streaming
  - o   virtual reality and augmented reality services

- o human-centric communications
- o eMBB provides mobile devices with fiber-optic bandwidth and speeds
- **Massive Machine-Type Communications—mMTO**
  - o small data volumes on an enormous scale
  - o low cost and complexity
  - o long battery life
  - o narrowband internet of things
  - o monitoring and automation of buildings and infrastructure
  - o tracking and fleet management
  - o smart agriculture
  - o logistics
  - o firmware updates
  - o smart cities
    - public safety
    - improve transportation

Challenges and Opportunities

Software-defined network slicing will enable service providers to offer distinct functional layers with different types and levels of 5G services to different groups of customers, each with different requirements, all over a shared physical resource.

For governments, hospitals, universities, businesses, and for service providers, the architecture of communications networks is evolving, but so are the business models, the business cases, the future customer requirements, and the new array of wireless 5G devices that will be needed.

What will customers be willing to pay for new 5G services versus 4G? With evolving business models, how do service providers calculate a return on investment in upgrading to 5G? Will the FCC lower the barriers to encourage small cell deployment? Will there be federal, state, and local public funding?

Over the next few years, 5G deployment will be about investing, piloting, prototyping, testing, learning, and discovering the future of 5G wireless communications.

CHAPTER 11

Cybersecurity

The FIDO Alliance—Solutions in the Pipeline

Cybersecurity is about protecting society as a whole, the nation's increasingly complex and interconnected vital economic infrastructures, government agencies, industries, businesses, hospitals, and individuals who depend on computers, software applications, and networks from attacks by hostile actors.

From cyber terrorism to malware for hire, the frequency, sophistication, and tactics are growing: Network security attacks. Questionable cloud and software vendor security. Broken access, identity, privilege, and session management. Removable media threats, firewalls, and security software misconfigurations. All organizations are at risk of data exfiltration, unauthorized access to critical data.

Cybersecurity can no longer be a technical support function. Strategy, decisions, priorities, and resources will require new skills, new perspectives, and new leadership.

- How do we protect the organization's reputation?
- How do we assess our cybersecurity vulnerabilities?
- How do we assess the risks of cloud computing, software as a service, and email/message service providers?
  - o How can we determine the risks of third- and fourth-party providers?
- Is it possible to secure, end to end, every device, every network connection, and every workload/ application?
- Given the highly specialized skills involved, where do we find proven security experience and talent?

Studies show that the cost per data breach is higher with the extensive use of mobile devices, migration of applications and data, third-party involvement, and regulatory compliance failures.

On the other hand, investments in cybersecurity can reduce the cost per data breach.

- governance programs
  - o audit committees
  - o certified internal auditors
- managed security services
- threat intelligence platforms
- employee training and education
- extensive use of encryption
- disaster recovery management
- security information and event management
  - o AI security analytics
- a fully functional cybersecurity response team

Next to the CEO, one of the most critical leadership positions in the organization may be the chief security officer (CSO). The chief security officer generally has the responsibility for the organization's governance, risk assessment, risk management, and government compliance programs.

The CSO needs to recruit and lead a team with the skills to defend the organization's cyberscape vulnerabilities:

✓ The unauthorized access, retrieval, modification, or destruction of proprietary data.
✓ Ensuring that all critical data is securely backed up, ready to be restored if needed.

Given the business continuity and reputation risks associated with a significant breach of data security, the CEO and the board of directors should not underestimate the challenge of building an effective cybersecurity team. The global demand for certified cybersecurity skills far exceeds the available talent. Begin building the security team by certifying several of the organization's IT professionals.

Mapping the cyberscape and the underlying infrastructures can help paint a picture of society's exposure to cyber attacks.

The cybercrime industry's hostile actors have a wide range of exploit techniques at their disposal to steal information and money and disrupt the delivery of essential services. Their attacks can either be targeted or opportunistic, and they frequently combine different intrusion tools to compromise and gain access to their targets.

Hostile Actors—The Objectives

- the nation-states, intellectual property, state secrets, espionage
- organize crime, financial gain, treasure
- terrorist groups, terrorism
- professional hackers, for hire, hacking as a business
- hacktivists, publicity, leak sensitive information
- industrial espionage, intellectual property
- disaffected insiders—disgruntled employees, contractors, whistleblowers
- amateur hackers—learning, thrills, bug hunting
- attackers relying on human error

For employees and individual consumers, the internet offers instant access to information, knowledge, learning, shopping, and entertainment. However, the web carries significant privacy and security risks.

For government agencies and business organizations, the cyberscape infrastructure is significantly more diverse, with many more vulnerabilities, risks, and threats.

Cyberscape Infrastructure Vulnerabilities

Computers

Think of a computer as a series of layers. At the bottom is the hardware. Next is the basic input-output system program, known as firmware, which connects and defines the hardware to the operating system software. The top layer is the user application software.

Internet

Think of the internet is having three components. First is the hardware—the cables, transmission lines, routers, servers, nodes, radios, cell towers, and satellites that together rout the traffic through a network of networks. The second component is the internet protocols (IP), the communications protocol or language used to exchange messages between computers on the internet. And finally, the software for using and managing the network.

Organizations

For organizations, the IT infrastructure consists of routers, network communication services, and network software: operating systems, firewalls, and network security applications. It functions as the foundation for internal and external communication, storage, processing, and analysis of data.

The IT infrastructure may be composed of physical or virtual resources, centralized in the organization's data center or hosted in several data centers by a third-party or cloud service provider.

Software

Software, computer instructions, can be divided into three categories. Systems software includes the operating system and the utilities that support the computer functions. Application software programs support the end users. Software as a Service is a method where applications software is hosted on a cloud vendor's computer and made available to customers over the public internet or a VPN, a virtual private network.

All hardware needs software to function, but there is no such thing as bug-free, vulnerability-free software. The number of exploitable bugs is directly proportional to the number of lines of code in a given cyberscape infrastructure.

For example, on a laptop, the operating system alone can consist of millions of lines of code. Coding flaws accumulate from one update generation to another, becoming increasingly difficult to find and fix.

Murphy's Law of Software Debugging

- Software doesn't become more reliable as it is debugged; the bugs get harder to find.
- Bugs appear in one part of a program when another unrelated area is modified.
- Patching a piece of software replaces old bugs with new bugs.
- The amount of time required to debug software is directly proportional to the amount of user input.
- There's an inverse relationship between the organization's hierarchy and its understanding of computers systems.

The most straightforward part of software quality assurance testing is proving that the code performs all the functions that the user or users specified and expect. The extremely challenging and sometimes impossible part of QA is the ability to find all the flaws, vulnerabilities, security bugs, and the logic paths not specified in the design and not expected.

Simply put, all software can be hacked.

Finding Hackable Software Bugs

All programs have vulnerabilities; they just have not been found yet. High-tech companies like Google, Apple, and Facebook, as well as government agencies, including the Department of Defense, offer bug bounty programs to reward hackers that find security vulnerabilities in software, websites, and web applications before the cybercriminals do.

In 2016, companies and agencies paid out $6.3 million for 52,000 discovered vulnerabilities, according to Bugcrowd, a bug bounty resource. To be a bug hunter, you need programming skills, an understanding of penetration testing, and access to software tools.

Exploiting Vulnerabilities

An exploit targets security vulnerabilities in the cyber-scape infrastructure. An exploit kit is a malware program that manages multiple exploits. For example, an exploit could be a website uniquely crafted to appear legitimate. Once a computer or mobile device opens the hacker's website, the exploit kit runs, probing the device for vulnerabilities. If successful, the cybercriminals then download and embed malware or other malicious software programs to the compromised device.

Sometimes the exploit kit incorporates tracking mechanisms to gather information about search activities, operating system, browser, and the software that was exploited. The exploit kit is frequently used by cybercriminals to gain a foothold on a device, which an attacker can then use in the future.

Two critical processor flaws used in today's desktops, mobile devices, personal computers, and cloud computing networks have recently been discovered. These processor vulnerabilities offer hackers an opening to steal cryptographic keys, passwords, and other sensitive data that is being processed by the chipset.

Also, a severe firmware security flaw has been found in specific vendor's trusted platform module (TPM) chipsets. The TPM is the cryptoprocessors that securely store critical data such as passwords, biometric authenticators, certificates, and encryption keys.

Embedded Malware

- tracks your keystrokes and sends the information to the hackers
- scans your documents, searching with keywords
- redirects your web searches to a malicious website
- keeps changing, so that succeeding versions are difficult to find
- mobile code embedded in the email, email attachments, and websites

Advanced Persistent Threats

- steady, sophisticated, and targeting specific entities
- hiding, undiscovered, over an extended period
- orchestrated with external command and control systems

- monitoring and extracting privileged data
- placing customized malware on multiple computers

For government agencies and business organizations, the cyberscape infrastructures can be diverse and complicated. They access application software and data from in-house data centers or cloud vendors' computers, or both, through wired and wireless networks. Connecting through numerous endpoint devices—smartphones, desktops, laptops, and workstations—is consequentially more complex, with many more vulnerabilities, risks, and threats.

However, no two cyberscape infrastructures are the same, and as a result, no two solutions are the same. The vulnerabilities, threats, and risks are all unique and different.

Cybersecurity Management—Highly Challenging

The following are some reasons cybersecurity management is highly challenging:

- the growing sophistication and the indistinguishable remote nature of the cyber attacks

- the vulnerabilities of software, cloud computing, and wireless networks
- the ever-increasing number of connected devices
- the shortage of cybersecurity talent and expertise
- the state, federal, and international regulatory compliance concerns
- the number and total cost of data breaches
- no metrics for measuring cybersecurity risks

Laws and Regulations

There are different approaches used by states, the federal government, and international agencies to ensure compliance with their regulatory obligations.

The principles-based regulatory approach articulates the objectives and principles that an organization is expected to follow, without describing the detailed systems design for compliance.

In the prescriptive or rule-based approach, the compliance process is stipulated in detail—what the regulated entity must do, or cannot do, including recommendations for cybersecurity best practices.

Some regulatory agencies combine the prescriptive/rule-based and the principal-based approach with an emphasis on corporate governance. Organizations are required to install specific security measures within an overall framework that ensures management accountability for regulatory compliance.

The General Data Protection Regulation (GDPR) legislation from the European Union is a prescriptive/rule-based approach, protecting EU residents' personal data without regard to whether the data resides in the EU or not. All companies, including US companies, must comply with the GDPR regulatory guidelines or face substantial financial penalties.

In the United States, the prescriptive/rule-based approach for cybersecurity is used by the Federal Banking Agency, the Federal Reserve Board, the Office of the Comptroller of the Currency, and the Federal Deposit Insurance Corporation.

The increasing number of well-publicized data breaches has led to calls in the US for legislation and regulations for enhanced cybersecurity measures that address the risks posed by cybercriminals. In 2017, US states introduced 240 breach notification bills and resolutions requiring that customers be notified if their personal information was breached. California alone has added twenty-five privacy and data security laws.

New York Department of Financial Services has mandated that banks, insurance companies, and financial institutions doing business in the state comply with specific requirements.

In general, the total cost per data breach is lower when regulatory agencies use a prescriptive/rule-based approach to cybersecurity compliance.

Increasing Complexity

The majority of enterprises are implementing public and private multicloud strategies. They cite the advantages of scalability, costs, support for multiple lines of business, and connections to various cloud service providers.

At the same time, they are making significant investments in layers of cybersecurity technologies designed to find and defend against malicious activities embedded in the network traffic. However, this added complexity has increased their exposure to cybersecurity risks. They remain vulnerable, with data breaches and compromises more prevalent than ever.

Cybersecurity threats were not a consideration when the internet was conceived. Over time, we've learned that adding incremental cybersecurity solutions from different vendors, not designed to interoperate, have led to gaps and vulnerabilities that can be exploited. Security must be designed in, not added on.

Globally, cybersecurity threats pass through the internet backbone communications unchallenged. As a result, today's internet favors the cybercriminals, threatening individuals, organizations, and governments worldwide.

Mobile traffic is growing, hiding billions of malware, ransomware, and spyware attacks. Encrypted attacks cannot be decrypted and inspected with artificial intelligence. The result is cyber espionage and national security risks.

Something Must Change

We are all overloaded with passwords (memorized secrets); too many to remember, they can be hacked, stolen from the server, and entered into untrusted websites/apps. They are inconvenient, time-consuming, and frustrating.

In our network-based digital economy, virtually everything is interconnected, and everything is at risk of a cyber attack. Adding layer after layer of security to our existing infrastructures is not working.

The use of artificial intelligence to search for malicious traffic within the internet or when it reaches its target has been helpful but is not the long-term solution.

Hypertext transfer protocol (HTTP) is the traditional basis of data communications for the internet. Hackers present a clear danger to all HTTP connections between a web browser and a website since the data is plain text, not encrypted, and easily readable. Hypertext transfer protocol secure (HTTPS) is an encrypted and secure version of HTTP, which means that if the connection is hacked, they would not be able to decrypt any of the data passing between the user and the website. Web browsers display a padlock icon in the address bar to show that the HTTPS connection is in effect.

Using encrypted connections between browsers and websites is essential but is not a long-term solution. Criminal hackers have been known to exploit HTTPS to gain trust with users.

With an increase in unauthorized access attempts and failed user logins, data breaches are becoming more common, regulatory compliance more prescriptive, and the board of directors more concerned. We need to think differently about cybersecurity, rethink how the internet works, and deal with cyber threats before they enter the internet, not afterward.

It is the author's view that the only long-term answer is to stop the invaders at the front gate. Once they get in, we can slow them down but not eliminate the threats.

When we use our network of streets and highways, our vehicles are inspected, registered, and licensed. All drivers must prove their identity, register, and carry a valid driver's license when operating a motor vehicle. Traffic violations may result in the loss of privileges.

The Cybersecurity Solutions

Identity and access management process is about defining and managing individual network users roles and access management privileges, ensuring that only registered users with trusted devices and software are granted access to online services, applications, and data assets and in the right context.

Facial recognition identity technology has already become the first step: unlocking a device, launching an app, or picking up messages.

The overall concept of identification and access management involves two interactive subsystems: authentication and governance management administration.

Authentication

The Fast Identity Online Alliance (FIDO) is a nonprofit organization with more than 250 members, including the leading technology providers and global brands, formed to address the issues of interoperability among available authentication technologies.

The FIDO Alliance authentication standards are being embraced by leading firms across the globe, such as Google, Amazon, Facebook, eBay, Dropbox, Bank of America, PayPal, Visa, Aetna, Intel Corporation, Samsung Electronics, Qualcomm, and American Express.

The FIDO Alliance recently announced nine more companies had become FIDO certified, including Acceptto, AirCUVE, Fishbag Technology, Jazz Networks, Gemalto, and Smart Technology Investment and Development. Also, FIDO announced that the number of certified devices supporting its Strong Authentication Standards now exceeds 465.

In each deployment of FIDO authentication standards, the end user does not need to understand how the process works, only that it is secure. With FIDO, the login experience is simple, and security is behind the scenes.

The mission of the Fast Identity Online Alliance is to redesign online user authentication.

The alliance is developing technical specifications for a password-less, scalable, open, and interoperable system for access management to authenticate online users. FIDO standards were built with the European Union GDPR "privacy by design" approach. FIDO standards work for both mobile and desktop devices.

- simpler—easily authenticated online services
  - o   stronger web multifactor authentication using:
    - ▪   something you know—secrets

- something you have—hardware key
- something you are—biometrics
- authenticators
    - bonded authenticators built directly into the access device, stored securely on the Trusted Platform Module (TPM 2.0)
    - roaming authenticators, physically independent of the access device
        - able to travel between FIDO credentialed devices
        - connected via USB, Bluetooth, or near-field communication (NFC)—Apple Pay, Samsung Pay, Google Pay, Fitbit Pay, bank mobile applications
- FIDO authentication standards are being implemented:
    - web browsers—Foxfire, Mozilla, Chrome, and Microsoft Edge
    - operating systems—Android and Windows 10

The 5G virtualization of networks and network functions will require strict isolation at multiple levels to ensure absolute security. As part of the FIDO Alliance, the Intel and Gemalto combined solution confirms that virtual functions and applications residing in network slices are protected and isolated.

The Trusted Computing Group is a nonprofit organization that publishes and maintains the Trusted Platform Module (TPM 2.0) specifications for PCs, tablets, or smartphones.

The TPM 2.0 security processor is tamper-resistant cryptographic hardware soldered to the motherboard.

The TPM 2.0 has some important capabilities:

- secure boot—defined and trusted configuration
- random number generation / cryptographic operations
- secure storage of encryption keys and other secret data/biometrics
- remote attestation
  - proved to a remote party that the operating system and application software are intact and trustworthy

Device FIDO Authentication—How It Works

- It is based upon proven public/private key cryptography.
  - The private key is secret and stored in the user's device (TPM 2.0).

- o The public encryption key is shared with the online service.
- User sign-on may involve swiping a finger, looking at a camera, speaking a phrase, or inserting a hardware key.
  - o Biometrics, if used, never leaves the device (TPM 2.0).
  - o No third-party protocols.
  - o No server-side secrets to steal.
- The device verifies the user and unlocks the second, secure private encryption key (TPM 2.0) to authenticate the user to the online service.
- Biometrics and cryptographic keys are never sent through the network (TPM 2.0).

Identity Governance and Administration

FIDO Alliance authentication supported by identity governance and administration systems (IGA) are designed to manage digital identity accounts across all networks, customers, employees, business partners, devices, and things.

Our legacy systems were designed to provide on-premises employees with access to the company's data processing systems. Today, the always-connected mobile workforce and multi device ownership need secure 24-7 wireless access.

A significant percentage of cybersecurity threats come from mobile devices gaining access to the organization's data using credentials stolen from customer devices. To mitigate the cybersecurity risks inherent in mobile devices, organizations are implementing identification governance and administration systems. Identity governance and administration systems, IGA, interacts with but is different from authentication systems. Identity and governance administration systems provide for identifying, authenticating, and authorizing employees, business partners, and customers to access the organization's applications and networks by associating rights and restrictions with an established identity. Identity governance and administration services provide the organization with the ability to define, enforce, review, and audit the organization's security policy, map results to compliance requirements, and audit user access. Different authentication user circumstances lead to unique identity and access management privileges. Authentication, identity governance, and administration of network user access for employees, business partners, and customers have proven to be very challenging.

Creating a Secure 5G Communications Network and Services Environment for the Future Internet

Over time and with much effort, an infinitely rich and secure 5G communications network will ensure that only the right individuals, using the right devices, with the right software, get the proper access to the right websites, applications, and data, and for the right reasons.

CONCLUSION

We are undergoing disruptive change, with no end in sight. We cannot escape, but we can adapt. It will take a profound commitment from everyone in the organization to learn to adjust to the constantly changing circumstances and conditions.

Becoming an adaptive organization is not about making a few minor adjustments to the way we do things. It is about the following:

- Adaptive leadership and followers
- Creating a team-based business model designed to experiment, prototype, learn and discover the future
- Investing in technology and talent
- Building a culture capable of adjusting to a constantly changing world
- Winning the competitive battle and not becoming obsolete

The world as we have known it is vanishing. Our cherished organizational traditions are no longer timeless and enduring; they are our heritage, our starting point for rediscovery and for creating the future.

When everything is changing, we need to think differently and rethink everything. It will not be an easy journey. However, by listening, asking, and answering questions, we can draw out ideas and underlying perspectives. Questions lead to answers, which lead to questions, which lead to solutions. If we are unwilling to be adaptive, we are likely to face insurmountable problems. However, with the right perspective, creativity, and determination, we can take the initiative and convert obstacles to opportunities.

Startup organizations are already applying the think-differently and rethink-everything ideas and concepts. There are no MBA case studies, and business schools are not teaching how to think differently and rethink everything. Organizations cannot wait for the status quo to work.

Our daughter, Shari, often tells her team, "If you want to be different, then do different, think different, and act differently."

ACKNOWLEDGMENTS

This book emerged from a journey that started in H. Ross Perot's office at Electronic Data Systems in Dallas, Texas. Ross was a graduate of the United States Naval Academy, and after leaving the navy in 1957, he became one of IBM's leading salesman. Ross started Electronic Data Systems (EDS) in 1962, offering long-term facilities management contracts for high-end Electronic Data Systems development, operations, and management.

I joined EDS as a senior systems engineer and the fortieth employee. At the time, I viewed myself as technical, with only limited supervisory experience. My first day on the job, Ross gave me a book by Joe Batten: *Developing a Tough-Minded Climate ... For Results.* He suggested that I read a chapter in the evening, and we would discuss the management concepts, philosophies, and ideas the next morning.

I'm deeply grateful and appreciative of Ross Perot's expert guidance, counsel, and leadership. Over the years, I've shared many of the business concepts and philosophies that I learned from Ross with our children and grandchildren, who have encouraged me to write a book.

My greatest thanks must go to my friends Bob Bergdoll, Don Stone, and Don Kirkpatrick, who provided a constant stream of good advice, counsel, and encouragement during this project.

I would also like to thank David Labno, chief executive officer of NeuroColor, for helping me understand the significant talent management opportunities available through personality assessments.

And finally, I would like to acknowledge the support and patience of my family: my wife, Jeanette; our children, Bobby, Dennis, Teri, Shari, and Michael; our grandchildren and sons-in-law Paul Antonissen and Leonard Scholl. This book would not have been possible without them.

INDEX

artificial intelligence (AI)
    as commonplace, 59
    investments in, 25
    as new technology, x
    Platform as a Service (PaaS) and,
        73, 81
    as reshaping talent management
        programs, 49
    use of to gain personalized in-
        sights about consumers,
        35–36
    use of to match people to
        jobs, 50
    use of to search for malicious
        traffic within internet, 109
assessment
    of natural competencies and po-
        tential, 44
    NeuroColor personality assess-
        ment, 18, 44
assets, investment in intangible as-
    sets, 25–29
AT&T, as communication service
    provider (CSP), 85, 88
authentication technologies, 111–115
autonomy of thought, 18
Azure (Microsoft), 66

B

baby boomers, retirement of, 39
bank mobile applications, as roam-
    ing authenticators, 113
Bank of America, FIDO Alliance
    authentication standards as em-
    braced by, 111
"Best Places to Work" (Glassdoor), 36
blockchain technology, 59, 75, 80

BlueMix (IBM), 66
bonded authenticators, 113
branding
    customer branding, 36, 53
    employer branding, 13, 38, 42,
        52–53
budget management, continuous
    budget management, 33–34
bug bounty programs, 101
bug hunter, 101
Bugcrowd, 101
business model
    adaptive business model, 6, 37
    design of, 31
    evolution of, 92
    planning process as historically
        defining, 30
    as at risk of digital disruption,
        54, 57
    team-based, 119
business units, 31

C

certified/credentialed devices,
    112, 113
change
    accelerating change, vii, viii, xi
    humans as remarkably adaptive
        to, 2
    as not optional, 60
    successful navigation of, xii
change agents, xii, 43, 60
chief artificial intelligence officer,
    7, 38
chief customer officer, 7
chief marketing officer, 38
chief project management officer, 32

Murphy's law of software debugging, 100–101
solutions, 110–114
something must change,
108–110

D

data breaches, 94, 95, 105, 106–107,
108, 110
Department of Defense, as offering
bug bounty programs, 101
device authentication, 114–115
devices
certified/credentialed, 112, 113
mobile, 79, 84, 87, 91, 94,
102, 116
digital disruption
forces of, 56
managing of, 54–56
opportunities and risks of, 57
risks from, 54
digital economy, network-based, 109
digital transformation
benefits of cloud computing services, 81
build digital transformation
(DX) team, 61–62
change is not optional, innovation not voluntary, 60
cloud computing, 76–78
cloud computing services, 65–66
cloud delivery models, 66–72
cloud vendor selection, 75–76
digital business journey, 62
digitally transformed economy, 79

downside of cloud computing
services, 82
get help, 60–61
infrastructure, 62–64
managing digital disruption,
54–56
questions for leadership and
board of directors, 57–59
three cloud services, 72–74
digital transformation (DX) team, 61
digitally transformed economy, 79
discovering, process of, 6
disruptive change
adaptive leadership as agents
of, 9
confronting reality of, 1–4, 30
constant battle to overcome, 25
as likely to accelerate, 43
no end of as in sight, 119
as prompting significant shifts
in corporate paradigms and
management strategies, 49
requirements of, 12
as undermining effectiveness of
strategic planning, 5
diversity, collective wisdom as com-
ing from greater diversity, 17
diversity of minds
benefits of, 49
embracing and celebrating of, 14
necessity for, 18
over ability, 17
diversity of talent, 58
dopamine, impact of on style of
thinking, 45, 46

P

PayPal, FIDO Alliance authentication standards as embraced by, 111
perception engine, of adaptive leader, 10
Perot, Ross, 11
personality factors, big five, 44
Personality Insights (IBM), 50
personality inventory. *See* NeuroColor Personality Assessment
planning process, historically, 30
Platform as a Service (PaaS), 73, 77
position descriptions, 48
potential
    assessment of, 44
    defined, 43
predictive project methodologies, 21
pricing, fundamental tenets of, 34
principles of management, as changing, 18
private clouds, 68–69, 70, 71, 78
progressive realization, defined, 6–7
project management. *See also* project managers
    chief project management officer, 32–33
    as core competency, 58
    culture of, 32
    skills and methodologies of, 19, 37
project managers
    requirements of, 22
    role of, 20, 23
project-managed meeting, 22, 23

projects
    adaptive versus predictive projects, 21
    defined, 20
    examples of, 20
public clouds, 66–68
public financial information, limitations of, 27
publicly held companies, number of (US), 28

Q

Qualcomm, FIDO Alliance authentication standards as embraced by, 111
quarterly earnings, rethinking of, 25–26

R

ransomware, 108
recruitment, of adaptive leaders, 43
regulation G, 28
regulatory compliance
    accountability for, 106
    as becoming more prescriptive, 110
    concerns of, 105
    failures in, 94
remote attestation, 114
retirements, loss of leadership and skills from, 39
revenue statement, as having lost much of its relevance, 27
RingCentral, as UCaaS specialist, 85
risk assessment, 95
risk management, 95

ABOUT THE AUTHOR

Bob Shafto has over thirty-five years of computers systems development, project, and executive management experience. After receiving his bachelor's degree in actuarial science from Drake University, Bob managed computer systems for Guarantee Mutual Life.

Mr. Shafto joined H. Ross Perot's Electronic Data Systems (EDS), where he was responsible for the development of computer systems for the insurance industry.

After joining New England Mutual Life Insurance Company as vice president and chief information officer (CIO), Mr. Shafto retired as chairman of the board and chief executive officer (CEO).

Mr. Shafto was a recipient of Drake University's Alumni Achievement Award.

Before his retirement in 1998, he was asked to speak at the MIT Sloan School of Business on the relationship between the CEO and the CIO.

CPSIA information can be obtained
at www.ICGtesting.com
Printed in the USA
FFHW011813270119
50263227-55266FF